W9-BRS-003

Happy reading!

In Style with Grandma Antoinette

♡ *Judith Caseley*

Judith Caseley

Tanglewood Press • Terre Haute, Indiana

With love to everyone at
Haircraft Forward, especially
the beautiful grandmothers:
Antoinette, Nilda, and Alice.

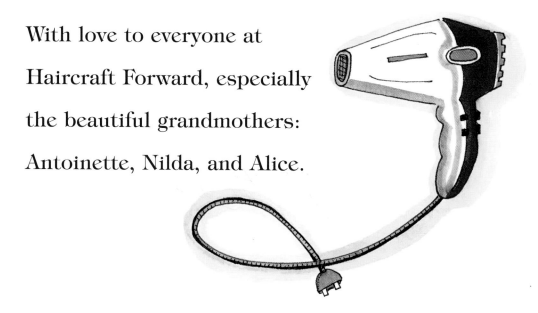

With special thanks to my models, Lena and Ariel.

Published by Tanglewood Press, LLC, November 2005.

©Judith Caseley 2005.
All rights reserved.

Neither this book nor any part may be reproduced or transmitted in any form or by any means, electronic or mechanical, including photocopying, microfilming, and recording, or by any information storage and retrieval system, without permission in writing from the publisher.

Designed by Amy Alick Perich.

Tanglewood Press, LLC
P. O. Box 3009
Terre Haute, IN 47803
www.tanglewoodbooks.com

Printed in the United States of America
10 9 8 7 6 5 4 3 2 1

ISBN 0-9749303-4-2
    978-0-9749303-4-3

When Mama told Rosie, "You're going to spend the day with Grandma," Rosie asked, "Will we go to the movies?"

"No," said Mama. "It will be better than that."

What could be better than watching a movie with Grandma, jumping up and down at the scary parts and spilling their popcorn?

"Will we sell lemonade and cookies and put the money in a jar?" Rosie asked.
"No," said Mama. "You'll have more fun than that."

What could be more fun than making lemonade with Grandma, collecting a jar full of quarters from people walking by?

"Will we go to the amusement park?" Rosie asked.

"No," said Mama, "but it will be just as exciting."

What could be as exciting as going to the amusement park, spinning around and around on the Cup and Saucer with Grandma, screaming as loudly as they could?

"I give up," said Rosie.

"You're going to spend the day with Grandma at her new job," said Mama.

"No, thanks," said Rosie. "Work isn't fun."

But Mama wouldn't take "no" for an answer, so she and

Rosie drove into town, parking in front of a shop called

Haircraft.

The receptionist announced into the intercom,

"Antoinette! Your new assistant has arrived!"

Grandma came running and gave Rosie a hug. Rosie and

Grandma said goodbye to Mama. Their day had begun!

Zelikha, the manicurist, was painting a lady's nails pearly pink with white tips. She smiled at Rosie and said, "Pick a color for later, honey."

wink of pink

pink parfait

wink of white

scarlet chiffon

Pretty Pink

berry blue

Purple Passion

Which nail polish would you choose?

golden glint wild watermelon mellow yellow pale pearl jelly red Emerald green

Then Rosie met a hair stylist named Giorgio. "Giorgio is coloring a client's hair from brown to blond," whispered Grandma.

Which hair color would you choose?

Rosie looked at the woman in Giorgio's chair. She reminded Rosie of a space creature. "She looks funny," Rosie whispered to Grandma Antoinette. "She'll look better later," Grandma whispered back.

"A shampoo for Antoinette!" Rosie heard over the intercom. At the back of the salon, Nilda put a plastic gown on Minnie. "I need a new lipstick!" Minnie told her.

"We'll find you a nice color later," said Nilda, helping Minnie to sit back with her head over the sink and turning on the water.

"Too hot!" shouted Minnie.

"I'm sorry," Nilda said. She squirted some shampoo onto Minnie's head and started scrubbing.

"Too hard!" said Minnie, and Nilda scrubbed more gently. Nilda wrapped a towel around Minnie's hair and settled her in Grandma's chair. She removed the towel and combed out Minnie's hair.

Which lipstick would you choose?

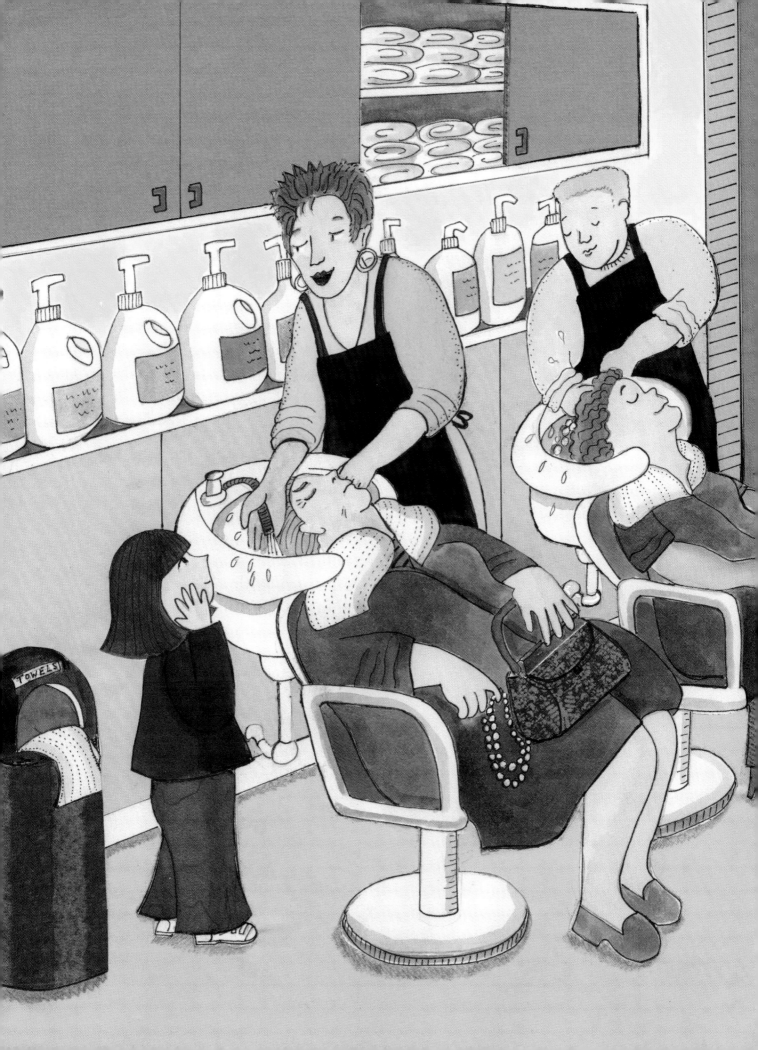

Grandma asked, "What are we doing today, Minnie?"

"Cut it short for summer," Minnie instructed, and Grandma snipped away. Then she took out a hair dryer and curled Minnie's hair with a big, round brush.

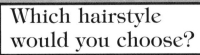
Which hairstyle would you choose?

"Can you bring me a drink, little girl?"
Minnie asked Rosie.
She gave Rosie money. Rosie put
the coins in the soda machine,
pressed a button for cola and
brought the can to Minnie.

"Keep the change," Minnie said.
"It's a tip," explained Grandma.
"When you do a good job, you get
a tip."

"Antoinette, can you come to the front desk?" Rosie heard.

She followed Grandma to the front of the salon, where a head of hair was floating through the air. Rosie hid her head while Grandma explained, "It's a wig on a mannequin head."

"I need my wig styled by the end of the day," said the lady, holding it.

"Come back in a few hours," Grandma replied, putting the wig at her station.

A woman burst through the door, yelling, "Please, can you help me? I dyed my hair by myself, and I look like a zebra!"

The little boy with her was jumping up and down, saying, "My mother's a zebra! Let's go to the zoo!"

"I can fix it," said Grandma, giving the lady a robe. Then Rosie and the boy, whose name was William, followed Grandma into the color room and watched her mix color.

Which animal would you choose?

Rosie wandered downstairs and heard a lady say, "Ouch!"
The sign on the door said "Waxing Room" and Rosie peeked
inside. Zelikha was pulling a piece of cloth off of a lady's legs.
"See how nice and smooth?" she said to Rosie. "Now we need
our privacy."

Rosie went back upstairs. Zelikha soon followed. "Let's get
started," she said. She smoothed lotion on Rosie's hands and
painted her nails red.

Rosie dried them under a machine with tiny fans that went on
and off when she stuck her fingers underneath it.

Which hand cream would you choose?

Rosie heard a ruckus at the front of the shop.

"Where's my wig?"

"Where's William?"

We need a search party for a boy named William and a wig!

They looked in the bathroom.

They checked in the office and inside the lunch room.

No wig. No William.

Two screaming ladies.

One worried Grandma.

Rosie wandered back downstairs. She knocked on the
door to the waxing room and opened it a little. A blond
lady was lying on the table with a towel covering her body.
She was snoring.

"Have you seen a little boy?" Rosie whispered. She
squinted her eyes, walked inside, and peered at the
sleeping blond.

It was William on the table, wearing the wig.

Rosie ran upstairs and told Grandma and the receptionist, who announced over the intercom:

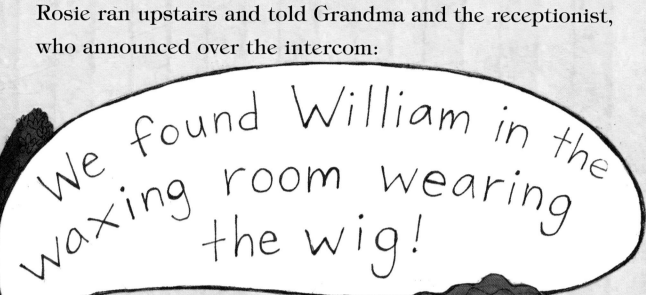

By the time Mama arrived, the excitement was over.
William, the zebra lady, and the wig had gone home.
Rosie hugged Mama and said, "You're early!"
"Was it as good as the movies?" Mama asked her.
"It was even better!" said Rosie. "I made tips!"
she said, pulling quarters and nickels and
dimes out of her pocket.
"Rosie saved the day," said Grandma, laughing.
She kissed Rosie goodbye.

On the way out, Rosie gave the receptionist a final message.

Then she and Mama left the salon.

Over the intercom, the receptionist announced,

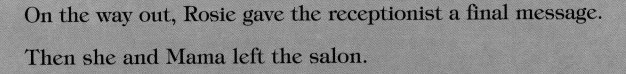

"Rosie says she loves you, Grandma Antoinette!"

Grandma heard it and smiled as she cut the next lady's hair.